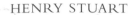

HENRY STUART

James I's eldest son, Henry, Prince of Wales, was quite unlike most of the Stuart family. He was a likeable, popular figure who did not seem to carry the family traits of arrogance and physical ungainliness. Unfortunately, he died of typhoid in 1612, leaving his younger brother, Charles, as heir to the throne. Had he lived, the course of British history might have been altogether different.

CHARLES'S CORONATION

Charles's coronation took place at Westminster Abbey on 2 February 1626. He had married Henrietta Maria the previous year, shortly after acceding to the throne, but it was not, initially, a love match. They seemed incompatible in almost every way. He was handsome, she was quite plain; she was a devout Catholic while he was a Protestant. She refused to attend Charles's Protestant coronation service.

ROYAL FAVOURITE

George Villiers had been a favourite at James I's court, dominating all matters of state. When James died he transferred his affections to the new king, Charles I. Created first Earl, and later Duke, of Buckingham, Villiers became Charles's most trusted advisor. The king was devastated when Villiers was assassinated in 1628 and was reconciled to his wife, who showed great compassion. Up until then the two had not been particularly fond of one another, but a genuine love seems then to have developed.

FASTIDIOUS APPEARANCE

Charles was a very fastidious person, always conscious of his appearance. Unlike his father (who is supposed never to have washed), Charles paid considerable attention to his personal hygiene. He liked to have his hair, wigs and beard carefully trimmed and styled by a barber, using similar equipment to that shown here.

THE YOUNG CHARLES

When he was

Charles came to the throne at 25 years of age. A shy man of diminutive stature (some accounts state he was just under 1.5 metres tall), he was also very intelligent and a great patron of the arts. He displayed a dignified air and good manners, far removed from the appalling personal habits of his father, James I. Charles was a reserved and very private man and the populace never really took him to their hearts. This, coupled with the Stuart family belief in the 'Divine Right of Kings', ensured that later on in his reign he became very unpopular, almost destined for the collision course with Parliament that led to the Civil War. In Scotland the monarchy still retained more of its absolute power, but in England this had been gradually whittled away.

'BABY CHARLES'

Charles was born on 19 November 1600 at Dunfermline Palace, Fife. He was the second son of James I and Anne of Denmark and so not born to be king. He inherited his father's lack of confidence and had a slight speech impediment; when nervous, he stammered. He was a sickly child, devoted to his brother Henry and sister Elizabeth. He was raised in seclusion and was referred to constantly by his father as *'baby Charles'*.

THE YOUNG KING

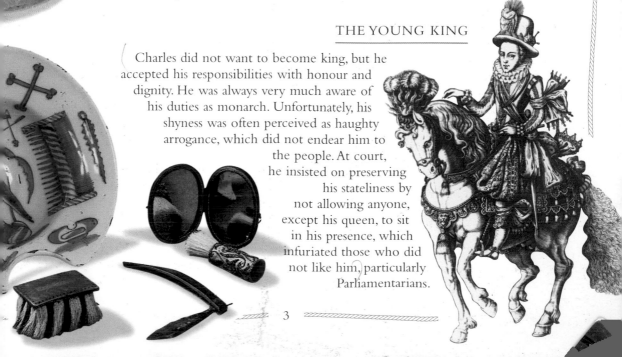

Charles did not want to become king, but he accepted his responsibilities with honour and dignity. He was always very much aware of his duties as monarch. Unfortunately, his shyness was often perceived as haughty arrogance, which did not endear him to the people. At court, he insisted on preserving his stateliness by not allowing anyone, except his queen, to sit in his presence, which infuriated those who did not like him, particularly Parliamentarians.

SCOTTISH DESCENT

On 23 November 1589, James VI married Anne of Denmark in Oslo and together they had nine children. It was a marriage of convenience that did not endear the king to his new English subjects.

The Stuarts were one of the most powerful royal families ever to rule Scotland. The first Stuart monarch was Robert II, formerly the High Steward of Scotland and Robert Bruce's grandson. They were an ambitious family who were also great patrons of the arts and elevated Scotland to the forefront of artistic and cultural development in Europe. The Stuarts were the last royal dynasty to rule an independent Scotland and were also distant relatives of the Tudors. James VI of Scotland (who became James I of England) was the great-grandson of Henry VIII's sister Margaret Tudor, who had married James IV of Scotland. When Elizabeth I of England died in 1603, her closest living relative was James VI (Stuart), King of Scotland, who was invited to take the English throne and so united the crowns of the two countries.

MARY QUEEN OF SCOTS (1542-67)

Mary was just one week old when she succeeded to the throne in 1542. In 1548 she was sent to France where she was brought up by her mother's family. In 1558 she married the French Dauphin and became, briefly, Queen of France when he became King as Francis II. Francis died in 1560 and Mary returned to Scotland the following year. She later married her cousin Henry, Lord Darnley, and became implicated in a plot to seize the throne of England from Elizabeth I, another of her cousins. She was arrested for treason and imprisoned by Elizabeth for 19 years, before being executed in 1587.

'DIVINE RIGHT OF KINGS'

Charles inherited his father's belief in the 'Divine Right of Kings'; a doctrine upheld by the entire Stuart dynasty. They believed in the theory that kings were chosen by God to rule and that only God could overrule them. Charles also believed that he alone had the right to make and unmake laws and to oppose his will was a sin against God.

ROYAL PALACE

Stirling Castle stands at the gateway to the Highlands and was always considered the most vital possession during Scotland's wars of independence. It dates from at least the 11th century, but the earliest part of the castle to survive dates from the 15th century, when the Stuarts converted the medieval fortress into a magnificent royal palace.

STUART FAMILY TREE

Robert II (1371-90)

Robert III (1390-1406)

James I (1406-37)

James II (1437-60)

James III (1460-88)

James IV (1488-1513)

James V (1513-42)

Mary Queen of Scots (1542-67)

James VI (1567-1625)
(became James I of England - 1603-25)

Charles I (1625-1649)

JAMES VI OF SCOTLAND
(James I of England)

James VI succeeded to the Scottish throne in 1567 when his mother, Mary Queen of Scots, was arrested. He was just one year old and Scotland was ruled during his minority by a regent. In 1603 he succeeded to the English throne on the death of Elizabeth.

STONE OF SCONE

Traditionally, the kings of Scotland had for centuries been crowned at Scone Abbey. The ceremonial coronation stone (a large, rectangular boulder believed to date from prehistoric times), formerly kept at the Abbey, was seized by Edward I (of England) in 1296 when he declared himself king of Scotland. It was taken to Westminster, where it was placed beneath the coronation throne (shown here). It remained in London for 700 years before being returned to Edinburgh in 1996.

FAMILY LIFE

FAMILY ALBUM

This view shows two of Charles's daughters, the princesses Elizabeth and Anne. It comes from a portrait by the court painter, Van Dyck, who made many portraits of the royal family in everyday poses, and dates from 1637.

Charles was never happier than when he was surrounded by his family. Himself one of nine children, Charles had nine children of his own with his wife Henrietta Maria. It was in the privacy of the royal palaces that Charles really came into his own, presenting, by all accounts, an altogether different persona to that given in public. When carrying out his official duties he often over-compensated for his shyness and lack of confidence, but in private he could be more relaxed. Always a very gentle man, it was said that he never '*violated a woman, struck a man, or spoke an evil word.*'

JAMES II

Charles's second son, James, had converted to Catholicism in the 1660s and Parliament tried to prevent him from succeeding to the throne. He openly declared his intention to restore Catholicism to England. In 1688, when faced with a series of demands by Parliament to prevent this, he chose to abdicate and went into exile in France. The throne passed, jointly, to his daughter Mary and son-in-law William of Orange, the Dutch ruler.

DEVOUTLY RELIGIOUS

Charles was a very pious man and although devoted to the Anglican Church, he did not approve of the new Puritan movement favoured by Parliament. He appointed his own 'High Churchmen', the most eminent being Archbishop William Laud. Because Henrietta was a staunch Catholic, Charles was quite lenient towards Catholics and introduced, through Laud, certain elements of the papal masses into Church of England services, which caused a great deal of criticism.

FAMILY MAN

Whenever possible, Charles liked to spend time with his wife and children and liked nothing better than to play games with them in the royal nursery. He felt it was important that his children were aware of the full circumstances leading up to his trial (and eventual execution) and insisted that they visit him whenever possible throughout his imprisonment.

BORN TO BE KING

Charles's eldest son, Charles II, was born in 1630. Following his father's execution, Charles continued to fight against Parliament, but eventually lost to Cromwell at the Battle of Worcester in 1651 and fled to France in exile. In 1660 he was asked by Parliament to return to England as king. He acknowledged having 14 illegitimate children by his various mistresses, but none by his wife, so when he died in 1685 the throne passed to his younger brother, James.

QUEEN HENRIETTA MARIA

James I had originally tried to arrange a marriage for Charles with the crown princess of Spain to ensure peace between the two countries, but the plans were thwarted by politicians. Instead, Charles married Henrietta Maria, the 16-year-old daughter of the French king, Henry I. Charles found Henrietta unattractive, with her buck teeth and bulbous eyes, but when George Villiers was assassinated in 1628, he turned to her for comfort. They henceforth became a devoted couple and she actively supported him throughout his confrontation with Parliament. After her husband's execution in 1649 she returned, heartbroken, to her native France, where she died in 1669.

CHARLES I & CROMWELL TIME LINE

~1599~
Oliver Cromwell born

~1600~
Charles I born

~1603~
James VI of Scotland becomes first Stuart king of England as James I

Sir Walter Raleigh arrested for treason

~1604~
James commissions new English translation of Bible

~1605~
Gunpowder Plot; a Catholic attempt to blow up Parliament

LIFE IN STUART BRITAIN

WATER SUPPLIES

Fresh drinking water was difficult to obtain. In towns, most people bought their supplies from water-carriers who transported water in from the country. Communal wells were also common in towns, but the supplies were often contaminated, causing typhoid and cholera.

The Stuart age was a period of great change. Improved methods of agriculture meant that fewer people were needed to work the land. Many peasants were evicted from their farms, the majority of whom moved to the towns in search of work. This resulted in serious overcrowding in the towns, which in turn led to outbreaks of disease. Fire was one of the biggest risks as most buildings were made of wood and thatch. Streets were narrow, which allowed fire to spread quickly, as happened in the Great Fire of London, which changed the architectural landscape of this great city.

LIFE FOR THE RICH

A growing number of people became very wealthy indeed during this period, mostly as a result of increased foreign trade and exploitation as Britain's empire began to grow. Many nobles replaced their austere castles with magnificent mansions, preferring light, airy rooms and sparing no expense on fine decorations and furnishings.

UNHEALTHY LIFESTYLE

Periodic outbreaks of the Bubonic Plague had been a problem since the 14th century, but that which occurred in the 1660s was one of the worst on record. Over 100,000 Londoners died in the 1665 outbreak alone. Diseases such as plague were seen by many (especially the Puritans) as divine punishment from God. Child mortality was high; over half those born died within their first year. Only one person in 10 could expect to reach the age of 40.

PASTIMES

Although life was hard in Stuart times and annual summer holidays were unheard of, there were a number of official 'holy-days', when no-one was expected to work. People played games for fun, rather than competitive sports. The theatre was popular with people of all classes. The rich preferred masques (a combination of music, drama and dance) while the poor opted for bawdy plays.

GREAT DESIGNS

Inigo Jones was another artistic genius who received the support and patronage of Charles I. Born in London in 1573 he came to prominence by designing elaborate stage sets and costumes for masques. He was also a leading architect. He studied in Italy and introduced many classical themes into English architecture, greatly influencing Sir Christopher Wren. Two of his most celebrated works are the Banqueting House in Whitehall (rebuilt after a disastrous fire in 1619) and the Queen's House at Greenwich (shown left), commissioned by James I as an out-of-town residence for Charles's mother. Jones incurred the wrath of Cromwell and other Puritans because of his extravagant designs and died two years after Charles's execution.

BEN JONSON (1572-1637)

Ben Jonson was a playwright who specialized in writing masques, a favourite form of entertainment at Charles's court. Masques originated in 14th-century Europe and were frowned upon by the Puritans for their supposed debauched behaviour. They were banned altogether during the years of the Commonwealth.

VAN DYCK (1599-1641)

Anthony Van Dyck came from the Spanish Netherlands, an area of Europe we now know as Belgium. He studied art under the great master Rubens and quickly became his star pupil. When Charles became king he invited Van Dyck to settle in England, offering him a knighthood and an annual pension of £200, an unprecedented sum for the times. He moved to England in 1629 and remained there until his death in 1641.

RUBENS (1577-1640)

Sir Peter Paul Rubens was one of the most eminent painters and designers of the time. He was born in Flanders (now Belgium) and painted portraits for most of the royal families of Europe as well as religious subjects like the apostle, Simon (shown here). In 1635 Charles I commissioned him to paint the ceilings for the newly completed Banqueting House in Whitehall.

PATRON OF THE ARTS

Charles I was a true patron of the arts and, in addition to acquiring a vast personal collection of some 1,400 paintings and 400 pieces of sculpture, he also patronized and encouraged the leading artists and architects of the day. It was his avowed intention to create the finest and most civilized court in Europe. Charles and his wife, Henrietta, presided over a sumptuous world of banquets, balls and masques; a world of elegance and refinement, which was perfectly captured by Van Dyck, the most eminent of the court painters, and other great artists of the time. By promoting the arts, Charles sought to lift himself out of the shadow of the turbulent Middle Ages and to establish England as the centre of world culture.

VISIONARY POET

John Milton was born in 1608 and although he represented the spirit of the age with his deeply religious poetry, his political views put him at odds with Charles. He was a devout Puritan and became the Commonwealth's semi-official spokesman after the king's execution. His most celebrated works were *Paradise Lost* and *Paradise Regained,* which express his disillusionment with the politics of the day.

TRIPLE PORTRAIT

This unique triple portrait of Charles I was painted by Carlo Maratti in the style of Van Dyck. It was used by the sculptor Bernini when he created a bust of the king. It captures, perhaps more than any other portrait, the dignified, almost melancholic nature of the king's complex personality.

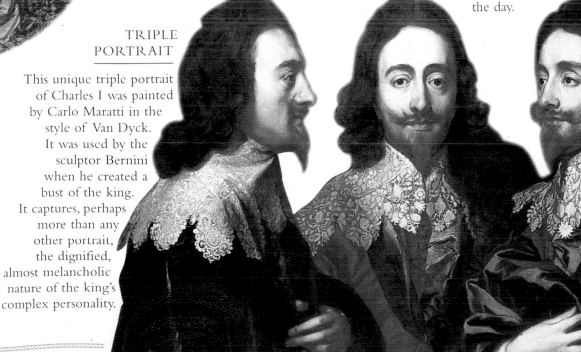

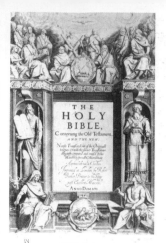

KING JAMES BIBLE

In 1604 Charles's father, James I, set 54 scholars to work on a new translation of the Holy Bible. It was published in 1611, using a vocabulary of just 5,000 words (one-third of that used by Shakespeare) to make it readable by all classes. The work of Anglican and Puritan ministers, James hoped the new Bible would unite the nation, but most Catholics disliked it, causing further religious division.

CHARLES & GOVERNMENT

Charles always had a somewhat fractious relationship with Parliament. At the root of the problem was his belief in the 'Divine Right of Kings' (see page 5) and his assertion that he should be allowed to rule without question or hindrance from anyone; least of all Parliament. He genuinely believed that a dictatorship was the only effective form of government, and the only one with the nation's interests at heart. Even a bad king, he argued, was better than a rabble of Parliamentarians who had not been schooled to care for a country in the same way as royalty. Moreover, he argued that a king exerted a controlling influence over individual excesses and was less susceptible to corruption. Whatever the rights and wrongs of his view, he was distinctly out of step with political thinking at the time, putting him on a collision course with Parliament.

RELATIONS WITH PARLIAMENT

Charles's character was a strange mixture that did not immediately endear him to others. In private he was polite, intelligent and kindly, yet in public he was often brusque, obstinate and impetuous, which put him at a disadvantage when dealing with officials, where a certain degree of tact and diplomacy was called for.

CHARLES ABOLISHES PARLIAMENT

Shortly after the death of his favourite, the Duke of Buckingham, Charles decided to dismiss Parliament. He had been on a collision course with Parliament for some time and was furious when, in 1628, he had been forced to acknowledge the Petition of Right (see page 15). When the agreement began to break down the following year, he dissolved Parliament altogether. He stubbornly refused to summon the House again and ruled on his own for 11 years.

THE 'LONG' & THE 'SHORT' OF IT

Charles's rule without Parliament became increasingly difficult as time went on. He had become virtually bankrupt and did not have control of his own army, so when rebellion broke out in Scotland he was unable to contain it and was forced to ask for assistance. Reluctantly, he recalled Parliament in 1640, but his first attempt was short-lived. He quarrelled with the members again and this Parliament was dismissed after just three weeks (known afterwards as the 'Short Parliament'). The situation worsened, however, and Charles was forced to recall Parliament again. This attempt was more successful and remained in office until 1653. It was afterwards known as the 'Long Parliament' and was finally dismissed by Oliver Cromwell for being incompetent.

THE KING RULES ALONE

Charles ruled alone, without Parliament, for a period of 11 years, between 1629-40. In order to overcome any political or religious opposition to his 'divine' rule, he gave additional power to the Court of Star Chamber (shown left) and the Court of High Commission (shown right), to support his actions. Both of these institutions served as a royal council and were made up of officials, justices and advisors. Their job was to administer any new laws passed, without corruption, to hear petitions and deal with complaints. When Parliament was recalled into office it was felt that the king had abused the power of these courts, so in 1641 both the Court of Star Chamber and Court of High Commission were abolished to prevent further corruption.

THE CIVIL WAR

CAUSES

ARCHBISHOP LAUD

William Laud was made Archbishop in 1633 to help endorse King Charles's policies and aroused the hatred of the Puritans with his antagonistic views. In 1637 he decided to impose the English Prayer Book on Scotland. The Scots were mostly Presbyterian (similar to the Puritans) and they hated bishops and prayer books, which they saw as 'popery'. These actions were a primary cause of the Civil War.

No single event can be cited as the direct cause of the Civil War; more, it was a gradual build up of mistrust between King and Parliament that finally came to a head when all other avenues of compromise had failed. With the growing strength of a democratic parliament in England and the medieval attitude of 'divine right' still ardently pursued by the Stuart monarchs, it was perhaps inevitable that the growing disagreement would ultimately lead to armed conflict. Charles hated the whole notion of parliaments, feeling that a dictatorial monarch, however bad, was preferable to the indecision of government by committee. Despite his shyness and retiring nature, Charles was often hot-headed and hasty. It was his ill-conceived attempt to arrest five members of Parliament that became the spark which ignited this tinderbox of discontent.

THE EARL OF STRAFFORD

Thomas Wentworth, Earl of Strafford, was a turncoat in the politics of the day who paid for his treachery with his life. He was instrumental in forcing Charles to agree to the Petition of Right. But then he switched loyalty to the king. Between 1633-40 he was Charles's deputy in Ireland, where he enforced a brutal regime against the Irish and soon became one of the most hated men in the country. As one of Charles's most ardent supporters, he aroused the anger of Parliament. They forced the king to sign a Bill of Attainder condemning Strafford to death. Charles had earlier promised to protect him, but Strafford magnanimously released the king from his obligations. He was executed on 12 May 1641.

SCOTTISH RIOTS

As a direct result of Laud's ill-conceived plan to impose the English Prayer Book on Scotland, the Scots erupted into open rebellion. The army was still controlled by Parliament, even though it had not been summoned for 11 years, and the King was unable to raise a sufficiently strong force to put down the riots. Reluctantly, in 1640, the virtually bankrupt Charles was forced to recall Parliament and ask for their help. It was an event that was to lead to the final confrontation between King and Parliament.

PETITION OF RIGHT

In February 1628, Parliament forced Charles to acknowledge the Petition of Right. He did so reluctantly because it gave Parliament certain liberties, whilst taking away the absolutism of royal power, but both Houses of Parliament were in agreement and Charles had to give it his assent. Its four main demands were that: taxation should be levied only with parliamentary consent; no-one should be jailed without trial; martial law should be abolished; and no troops should be billeted in private households. Charles was furious and it became the main bone of contention between King and Parliament.

CHARLES ARRESTS MPs

The actual event that started the Civil War occurred in January 1642 when Charles marched into the House of Commons and tried to arrest five leading MPs who seemed to oppose the king's every move. The MPs had been forewarned, however, and had already fled. Fearing he had himself gone too far, Charles fled for his own safety, to the North. The country began to divide itself between King and Parliament, and by August that same year he felt strong enough to raise his standard at Nottingham in defiance of Parliament: the Civil War had begun.

CHARLES CAPTURED

During Charles's period of imprisonment at Carisbrooke Castle, he enjoyed the privilege of freedom within its walls. He received frequent visitors, including his close family. His confinement gave him plenty of time to repent his actions, but he never faltered from his basic belief in his divine right to rule.

SCOTLAND'S DEFEAT

The Scots changed their allegiance several times through the war. At first they mostly supported Charles. However, the Presbyterian Church had gained much support in Scotland, which was a Protestant denomination similar to the Puritans in England, though even stricter. In 1646 Charles surrendered himself to the Scots, expecting compassion, but they handed him over to Cromwell in return for promises of religious freedom. After Charles's execution, however, Scotland proclaimed his son King, as Charles II. Cromwell defeated the Scots at the Battle of Dunbar in 1650. King Charles II himself was defeated at Worcester the following year and forced into exile.

BATTLE OF EDGEHILL

The Battle of Edgehill was the first major engagement of the Civil War. It was the first time since the Wars of the Roses, nearly 200 years before, that fellow countrymen had fought one another on English soil.

BATTLE OF NASEBY

The Battle of Naseby probably marked the real turning point in the conflict and effectively ended the war, in political terms. It took place in June 1645 and though the war dragged on until 1649, the Royalists were afterwards a spent force and the conclusion was inevitable. It was the first engagement of Parliament's New Model Army. At 15,000 strong and twice the size of the Royalist army, Parliament easily won.

THE CIVIL WAR

A NATION DIVIDED

W hen the Civil War broke out in 1642, there was no nationally organized army. Both the Royalist and Parliamentarian armies were comprised of ordinary men, mostly farmers or labourers with little or no military experience. They were also expected to provide their own weapons, which meant that both sides were initially very poorly equipped. The nation divided itself between supporters of the Royalist and Parliamentarian causes. Often families were divided in their loyalties, with brother fighting against brother and father against son. There was also a deeper, social divide; that of religion. Catholics tended to support the king, while Protestants, particularly Puritans, mostly supported Parliament.

BATTLE OF MARSTON MOOR

The Royalist cavalry, under the brilliant command of Prince Rupert, remained undefeated until 1644, at the Battle of Marston Moor. Cromwell won a resounding victory against the Royalists, earning Rupert's respect when he first coined the phrase 'ironsides' when describing the Parliamentarian troops. The battle was a turning point, giving Parliament a foothold in the North.

NEW FORTIFICATIONS

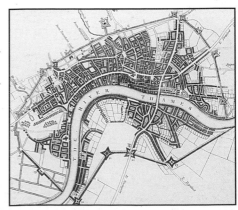

During the Civil War many of the great medieval castles of Britain were called into service. Because most were owned by noblemen who supported Charles, after the end of hostilities Parliament had many of their defences dismantled. All fortifications built after the Civil War had low, solid walls with angular or semi-circular bastions to carry heavy guns. These artillery style defences were built in many towns, including London, shown here.

THE CIVIL WAR
CAVALIERS & ROUNDHEADS

PRINCE RUPERT

In the early period of the Civil War, the Royalists were much better equipped and trained. They quickly gained the upper hand, thanks to the military skills of such loyal supporters as Prince Rupert, the German-born nephew of Charles I. Rupert came to his uncle's aid at the age of just 23. Although a scholarly man of science, he soon showed his prowess as an outstanding military commander. He specialized in lightning cavalry charges, in which his lightly-armed soldiers attacked the Parliamentarians at full gallop, making maximum use of the element of surprise.

In popular imagination the Civil War was fought between 'Cavaliers' and 'Roundheads', but these terms only came into common usage towards the end of the conflict. Historically, a cavalier was a courtier, a gentleman who attended the royal court and displayed a chivalrous attitude towards his fellow nobles, especially ladies. The clothes worn by Charles's supporters were not a uniform as such, but simply those worn by gentlemen at court. Most Parliamentary supporters were Puritans, who opted for simpler and plainer modes of dress. At the beginning of the war supporters of King or Parliament both wore similar clothes, distinguished only by coloured sashes or armbands. Only after Parliament organized the New Model Army in 1645 did the Parliamentarians adopt a standard uniform, comprising a red tunic, armoured breastplate and a round, metal helmet; hence the nickname 'Roundhead'.

SIR THOMAS FAIRFAX

One of the leading military commanders for Parliament was Sir Thomas Fairfax. He was appointed Lieutenant-General of the New Model Army in 1645 and, together with Oliver Cromwell, was largely responsible for Parliament's eventual victory. During the Civil War Leeds Castle, in Kent (above), was used as an arsenal for Parliament and so escaped the usual 'slighting' (dismantling) after the war. This magnificent castle later passed into the hands of the Fairfax family by marriage.

CAVALIERS &
ROUNDHEADS

The country
more-or-less sided itself
along a north–south
divide. Most of the
prosperous south-east,
including London
(perhaps surprisingly as it
was the seat of royalty),
supported Parliament.
Much of Wales, the north
and west, supported the king.
Initially, Scotland supported
the king, but with the
promise of religious reform,
many Scots switched their
allegiance to Parliament.
The Cavaliers were often
resplendent in their
flamboyant hats, knee-
length boots and fine tunics,
while the Roundheads
opted for a simpler uniform
of red tunics, leather over-
tunics, metal helmets and
breastplates. Both armies
comprised three main
elements: pikemen (foot
soldiers armed with pointed
pike staffs); musketeers
(using slow-
loading
musket
rifles) and
cavalrymen.
Armed with
swords and
pistols and
mounted on
horseback, the
cavalrymen
were the
cream of the
fighting force.

THE KING'S EXECUTION

In 1646 Charles was imprisoned by Cromwell. He managed
to escape but was soon recaptured and taken to Carisbrooke
Castle, on the Isle of Wight, where he remained for a year.
His supporters valiantly continued to fight, but it was by
now a lost cause. Charles had never wanted to go to war
with his fellow countrymen and seems to have genuinely
grieved for the loss of life in his name. Perhaps because
of this he made several tactical errors throughout the war
(one of the bloodiest in British history). Cromwell seized
upon his weaknesses and eventually won the day.
The king paid for his hesitation and clash of conscience
with his life. He was tried and executed for treason
within a week in January 1649.

CHARLES I & CROMWELL TIME LINE

~1611~
Authorized version of the Bible published

~1612~
Henry, Prince of Wales, dies

Charles becomes heir to throne

~1625~
James I dies

Charles succeeds to the throne

~1626~
Charles dissolves Parliament

~1628~
Duke of Buckingham is assassinated

Petition of Right issued, limiting royal power

Cromwell enters politics for first time

~1629~
Charles dissolves Parliament again

CARICATURE

Oliver Cromwell was neither a handsome nor a popular figure, even though he was generally acknowledged as a military genius and the man thought most capable of leading a nation that had been so bitterly divided. King Charles's trial and execution had been, to a large degree, unexpected. Most had expected the king simply to be deposed and imprisoned. His execution was certainly not met with the jubilation Parliament had expected. Even Cromwell seems to have been reluctant for things to have gone so far. Often the subject of derision, this caricature of Cromwell depicts him as a country squire, almost as a simpleton.

STATESMAN

Oliver Cromwell did not become a statesman through his military prowess alone, as is often supposed. Having already played an active role in local government, in 1628 he was chosen to be one of the representatives of Huntingdon in Parliament. It was the fourth year of Charles's reign and already the king had called three Parliaments. Cromwell's entry into politics thus coincided with the king's fall from popularity and the beginning of the real difficulties between King and State. In his first session in Parliament, Cromwell added his support to the passing of the Petition of Right, which guaranteed certain Parliamentary liberties and first gave Cromwell a thirst for political reform.

THE SITE OF CROMWELL'S BIRTH

Oliver Cromwell was born on 25 April 1599 and baptized four days later at the church of St. John the Baptist at Huntingdon. Very little is known about his early life. He was not a particularly academic child, though he did attend Cambridge University for about a year. He was forced to leave, without a degree, following the unexpected death of his father. Oliver was just 18 years old when he inherited the family property and the responsibility of looking after his mother and unmarried sisters.

OLIVER CROMWELL

EARLY LIFE

The Rump and dregs of the house of Com: remaining after the good members were purged out.

Oliver Cromwell's family were, in fact, of noble ancestry, though Oliver himself never inherited a title. His great-grandfather, Richard Cromwell, acquired vast properties in East Anglia and considerable wealth during the reign of Henry VIII, largely as a result of plundering the monasteries. Oliver's grandfather, Sir Henry Cromwell, was known as the 'Golden Knight', probably because of his immense wealth. Robert Cromwell, Oliver's father, inherited a small estate in Huntingdon. His wife Elizabeth was likewise descended from a noble family. Her father was Sir William Steward, who actually (somewhat ironically) claimed a very tenuous link to the Stuart royal family.

THE 'RUMP' PARLIAMENT

In 1640 Charles I had been forced to recall Parliament after 11 years of ruling without it. After a false start (known as the 'Short' Parliament) this Parliament sat for a total period of 13 years, afterwards known as the 'Long' Parliament. This Parliament had become very complacent during its 13 years of sitting and had become quite corrupt, earning it the derisory title, the 'Rump' Parliament because of its aversion to making important decisions. By 1653, fewer than 60 of its original 490 members remained. As Chairman, Cromwell eventually dismissed the 'Rump' Parliament the same year.

COUNCIL OF STATE

Following the execution of King Charles I, the remaining members of the Long Parliament decided to form a Council of State later in 1649. Oliver Cromwell was elected Chairman, but it proved a disappointment to him. He soon realized that many of its members were no more interested in parliamentary reform than the king himself had been and simply meant to further their own needs. They obstructed many of Cromwell's reforms, which prompted him to take matters into his own hands.

OLIVER CROMWELL
THE LATER YEARS

Towards the end of his life Cromwell became more and more disillusioned with life and he no longer fully held the conviction that his actions had been right. Parliament had several times proved itself to be as corrupt and as obstructive as the monarchy had ever been and he despaired that he had been unable to carry through the political reforms he had wanted. Furthermore, he knew that he had been ruling as virtual dictator, king in all but name, and that his dreams of a true democracy lay shattered. Britain's first brush with radical social reform had come to nothing. Although Cromwell himself was more liberal than many might suppose, the puritans who carried out many social reforms in his name were becoming hated by the people, who saw their reforms as stifling.

PURITANICAL GOVERNMENT

After he became Lord Protector, Cromwell called his first Parliament, which sat in 1654. The following year he dismissed it and ruled instead with the army. He divided the country into 11 districts, each one ruled by a Major-General.

MILITARY GENIUS

Cromwell was a self-taught soldier who learned his tactical skills by reading military accounts of great battles. At the outset of the Civil War he led a cavalry unit in East Anglia and quickly rose through the ranks. By 1644, he was appointed Lieutenant-General and the following year helped form the New Model Army. He was regarded throughout Europe as one of the leading commanders of his day.

CROMWELL OFFERED THE THRONE

In 1657 Cromwell was offered the crown of England by the Protectorate Parliament. By inviting him to become king, Parliament hoped to unite a country still deeply divided behind a common cause. Cromwell refused, saying that he was against the principle of hereditary rule. More importantly, perhaps, his own generals were also against the idea and threatened to revolt if he accepted. He was offered the crown several more times, but each time he refused.

BATTLE OF DUNBAR

The Civil War did not end completely with the execution of Charles I, as even Cromwell himself had expected. Hostilities dragged on intermittently for another two years. The Scots, dissatisfied at their treatment by Parliament, switched their allegiance once again and offered their support to the king's son, Charles II. Cromwell defeated them at the Battle of Dunbar in 1650, but they continued to support the Jacobite (Stuart) cause long after his death, finally ending at the Battle of Culloden in 1746.

CROMWELL DIES

Oliver Cromwell died on 3 September 1658. He had suffered attacks of colic, gout and recurring bouts of malaria throughout his life, the latter probably the cause of his death. It was rumoured that his Puritan beliefs would not allow physicians to administer a powder, brought back to Europe by Catholic priests from Spain, which might have treated his ailments. He was buried in state at Westminster Abbey, but his body was horrifically disinterred two years later and hanged at Tyburn by supporters of Charles II following his restoration. The severed head of his corpse was publicly displayed on the roof of Westminster Hall; an undignified end to a glittering career.

THE COMMONWEALTH

*F*ollowing the execution of King Charles I, Britain became, albeit briefly, a republic, but the new system of government was far from satisfactory. In many respects, it bore close similarities to the corrupt monarchical system it purported to replace. The dominant figure throughout was Oliver Cromwell. The period known as the Commonwealth can be divided into two distinct phases. The first, known as the 'Republic', spanned the period 1649-53 and was dominated by Cromwell's attempts to govern within the existing parliamentary framework. The second phase was known as the 'Protectorate', when Cromwell ruled as virtual dictator.

CROMWELL DISSOLVES PARLIAMENT

In 1653 Cromwell dismissed the Long Parliament because it had become corrupt and obstructive to his reforms. He declared himself Lord Protector and ruled with his New Model Army, a Council of 15 and a Parliament of 400. In all, three Protectorate Parliaments were called by Cromwell, but each was dismissed as it failed to live up to his ideals and blocked his plans for reform.

CROMWELL'S SUCCESSOR

When Oliver Cromwell died in 1658, aged 59, he was succeeded as Lord Protector by his son, Richard, despite his supposed aversion to hereditary rule. Known derisorily as 'Tumbledown Dick', he lacked his father's qualities of leadership and integrity. He did not want to be leader and accepted the position reluctantly. He was forced to resign the following year.

RESTORATION OF THE MONARCHY

To avert the prospect of another civil war, Parliament dismissed Richard Cromwell and invited Charles II to return as king from his exile in Holland. It was a popular decision for many people were growing dissatisfied with the strict and repressive lifestyle imposed by Puritan rule.

THE NEW MODEL ARMY

In February 1645, Parliament created a revolutionary new military concept by creating the New Model Army that was to change the course of the Civil War. The army was organized on a national basis and received regular wages, the first to do so. With its distinctive red coats (not shown here) it was also the first army in Britain to wear a standardized uniform.

Soldiers were well equipped and well trained. Officers were promoted to rank based on their abilities, rather than on their social standing.

PURITAN VALUES

Cromwell's Parliament introduced many laws to curb people's waywardness. Churches were stripped of all decoration and their interiors painted white to remove all idolatry. It became compulsory to attend church on Sundays, or face the stocks as punishment. Christmas and Easter celebrations were abolished, along with most forms of entertainment. Some Puritans became almost fanatical in their zeal for religious and political reform. One of these was Matthew Hopkins (right), the self-appointed 'Witchfinder General', who conducted a series of 'trials' between 1644-6 in which over 200 supposed witches were put to death at his instigation.

CHARLES I & CROMWELL TIME LINE

~1632~
Van Dyck invited to live in England as Court painter

~1637~
Charles tries to force new English Prayer Book on Scots

~1640~
Charles summons Parliament (known as Short Parliament), it lasts three weeks

~1641~
Star Chamber and Court of High Commission, abolished

~1642~
Charles tries unsuccessfully to arrest five MPs

Outbreak of Civil War

~1644~
Royalist army defeated at Marston Moor

INVENTIONS & DISCOVERIES

*H*ad the Stuarts ruled England during the Middle Ages, their story may well have been a happier one. As it was they came to the throne with antiquated ideas and philosophies which put them on a course bound for conflict. The 17th century was a period of great change, not just in political ideology, but in other important areas of thought, such as science and philosophy. The 'Renaissance' that had begun under the Tudors really came to fruition under the Stuarts. Several of the Stuart monarchs (James I, Charles I and Charles II in particular) promoted the development of art and the sciences, casting off many of the out-moded, medieval views of the world.

MICROSCOPIC DETAIL

In 1675 the Dutch naturalist Antoni van Leeuwenhoek developed the first single-lens microscope. For the first time scientists and botanists could see the natural world around

them in microscopic detail, objects too small to be seen with the human eye. As a result the study of medicine (in particular) progressed at an alarming rate. The microscope shown here is similar to one used by the physicist and inventor Robert Hooke. The accompanying illustrations show some of the organisms visible under the microscope for the first time.

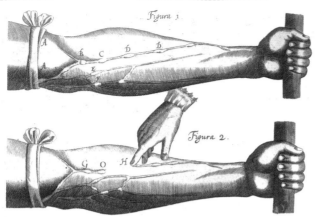

MEDICAL ADVANCES

The physician to King Charles I was William Harvey, a brilliant doctor who studied at the University of Padua, in Italy, and later joined the London College of Physicians. He completely revolutionized medical thought on the functions of the various parts of the human body. His special area of interest was the heart and it was he who first discovered the circulatory system of blood within the body. His discoveries made modern surgery techniques possible.

DISTANT VIEW

Sir Isaac Newton (1642-1727) was one of the greatest scientists of the Stuart age. He made major contributions to our understanding of mathematics (especially calculus) and physics, and first developed a theory of gravity. He also studied light and optics and developed the reflecting telescope, which greatly advanced our knowledge of the solar system and stars beyond. He developed a reflecting astronomical telescope which used mirrors rather than lenses to avoid the problem of light refraction.

BOYLE'S LAW

Robert Boyle (1627-91) was an Irish physicist and chemist who, again by scientific experiment, deduced various laws of physics (principally relating to temperature and gases) which were named after him.

WARS WITH EUROPE

HUGUENOT REFUGEES

The spread of Protestantism throughout Europe caused much unrest. In France over 60,000 Protestants (known as Huguenots) were forcibly converted to Catholicism in 1682. In 1685 the Edict of Nantes was revoked, which made it illegal for Protestants to freely practice religion. They were openly persecuted and many Huguenot refugees fled France and settled in England.

*O*ne of the most important consequences that arose from the years of bloody conflict in the Civil War was Britain's rise to power on the international stage. Throughout Europe, British commanders, such as Cromwell and Fairfax, were grudgingly regarded as the foremost military commanders and the emergence of the New Model Army held most of Britain's adversaries in awe. This Parliamentary army represented a whole new concept in military strategy, the like of which had not been seen since the Roman legions achieved similar success on the battlefield. At sea, such brilliant commanders as Robert Blake won numerous victories. Within two years of Cromwell's death the Commonwealth began to collapse, but Britain prospered under Charles II and continued to exert its influence abroad.

SIEGE OF DROGHEDA

Following Charles I's execution, the Irish and Scots led a combined rebellion against Parliament. For both countries it was seen as the ideal opportunity to remove, once and for all, English rule from their homelands. Cromwell sent a massive force against the Irish, defeating them at the sieges of Wexford and Drogheda in 1649.

WARS WITH FRANCE & SPAIN

Britain also found itself at war with France and Spain at various times throughout this period. Both countries, still largely Catholic and loyal to the Royalist cause, had leant their support to Charles during the course of the Civil War and Parliament wished to exert its new-found authority over them. Several of these skirmishes occurred in the colonies, where Britain was looking to build its dominions into an empire. Jamaica was successfully taken from the Spanish in 1655 and several victories were won against France in North America.

THE DUTCH WARS

In 1651 Parliament passed the Navigation Act which gave English merchant ships a monopoly over foreign imports and exports from English ports. This bolstered the English economy but caused almost immediate distress to the Dutch. War broke out with Holland in 1652, but the Dutch navy was defeated by the brilliant English commander, Robert Blake.

'SHIP MONEY'

'Ship Money' was a tax levied by the crown on coastal towns for the supply and maintenance of the Royal Navy. Throughout the 1630s the Navy had been allowed to run down, so Charles I extended the tax to inland towns to pay for new ships. This caused an uproar. In 1636 John Hampden, a Parliamentarian, refused to pay the tax. At a specially convened court the following year he was ordered to pay, but it was also acknowledged that the king had acted illegally, outside the provisions of the Petition of Right, and his authority was called into question. It proved to be the opening shot in the dispute between King and Parliament that eventually led to Civil War.

CHARLES I & CROMWELL TIME LINE

~1644~
Cromwell appointed Lieutenant General for all Parliamentary armies

~1645~
Parliament creates New Model Army

Royalists lose Battle of Naseby

~1646~
Charles surrenders to Scots, but they hand him over to Parliament

~1648~
Scots defeated at Preston

~1649~
Charles is tried and executed by beheading

Council of State appointed with Oliver Cromwell as Chairman

England declared a Republic

Irish Royalists defeated by Cromwell

~1650~
Scots Royalists defeated by Cromwell

~1651~
Scots Royalists led by Charles II (who claims the throne) defeated at Worcester

Charles II flees to France in exile

Navigation Act gives monopoly to English ships

DEATH WARRANT

This picture shows the death warrant of Charles I. It was signed by 59 specially chosen republicans and stated that the king should be executed by beheading. Many republicans shrank from signing the warrant, feeling that imprisonment was punishment enough. The news of Charles's impending execution sent shock waves throughout Europe.

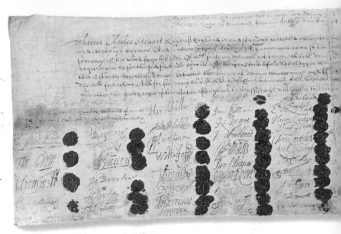

CHARLES I & CROMWELL TIME LINE

~1652~

First Dutch war breaks out

~1653~

Cromwell expels the Long (Rump) Parliament

Cromwell declares himself Lord Protector of England

~1654~

First Protectorate Parliament called

~1655~

Cromwell dismisses Parliament, rules with army and eleven Major-Generals

~1656~

Second Protectorate Parliament called

Rule by the 11 Major-Generals is abolished

~1657~

Cromwell refuses offer to take throne

~1658~

Cromwell dismisses Third Protectorate Parliament

Oliver Cromwell dies.

THE KING ON TRIAL

The trial of Charles I was held at Westminster Hall. It began on 20 January 1649 and lasted just one week. He reportedly said to friend

that if he had been unable to live as a king, he might at least die a gentleman. Charles refused to acknowledge the legality of the court and refused also to plead, stating: *'I do stand more for the liberty of my people than any that come here to be my pretended judges.'*

SAD FAREWELLS

Throughout his trial Charles had been confined to a house near to Westminster Palace, where he was allowed to spend time with his wife and children. His two eldest sons were safely exiled in France, but two of his younger children were also held as prisoners of Parliament; Henry, Duke of Gloucester and Princess Elizabeth. He gave Elizabeth a message for his wife, Henrietta Maria, to be passed on after his death, which stated that he had always thought of her and loved her to the end.

CHARLES I's IMPRISONMENT

Following Charles's defeat at the Battle of Naseby, in June 1645, the king fled to Scotland, but the Scots betrayed him and handed him over to Parliament. He managed to escape but was soon recaptured and, in November 1647, was imprisoned in the island fortress of Carisbrooke Castle. He enjoyed relative freedom there and negotiated with Parliament to secure his release. At the same time, however, he secretly organized an invasion of England by the Scottish army. They were defeated by Cromwell at Preston in August 1648, leaving the king at the mercy of Parliament.

THE RETURN OF THE MONARCHY

Charles I remains the only British monarch to have been formally charged with treason and executed. He was accused by Parliament of being a *'tyrant, traitor and murderer...and public enemy'*. Even after the Royalist cause had been lost, Charles stubbornly refused to accept defeat, to repent of his actions or to acknowledge republican authority. He also refused to alter his principle on either the monarchy or the Church, forcing some of Cromwell's more fanatical supporters to call for his execution. Charles rose magnificently to the occasion. Dressed entirely in black he remained dignified throughout the proceedings. His last words were: *'I needed not to have come here...I am the martyr of the people.'*

EXECUTION

Sentence was passed on Charles on 27 January 1649. He was given just three days to put his affairs in order before his execution on 30 January. The king's friend, Bishop Juxon, administered his last Holy Communion. Charles spent his last night at St. James's Palace, with his family, and at 10am the next morning he was escorted to Whitehall. The executio[n] place at 2pm axe fell, a around th his sev held a

A NEW KING

When Charles II returned to the English throne in 1660 public opinion had turned away from republican ideals. The surviving 41 republicans who had signed his father's death warrant were called to justice. Most of them fled abroad, or voluntarily surrendered, to escape execution, but 10 of the regicides refused to beg forgiveness. They were all tried and sentenced to death. The rotting bodies of Cromwell and two of his leading officers were also exhumed and hanged at Tyburn.

DID YOU KNOW?

That Charles I refused to show fear, even on the scaffold? Throughout the ordeal of his imprisonment and trial, Charles retained a dignified air and refused either to acknowledge his accusers or show fear of death. On the day of his execution, it was a cold January day and so that he would not shiver and give the impression of being afraid, he requested an extra shirt to keep him warm. The shirt can still be seen in the Museum of London today.

That the nursery rhyme 'Goosey, Goosey, Gander' refers to Cromwell? This well-known nursery rhyme is a direct reference to Cromwell and his Roundheads.

'Goosey, goosey, gander,
Whither shall I wander,
Upstairs and downstairs
And in my lady's chamber.
There I met an old man
Who would not say his prayers,
So I took him by the left leg
And threw him down the stairs.'

Soldiers in Cromwell's New Model Army were noted for their 'goose-stepping' march. After the Civil War they searched the houses of all known Royalist and Catholic sympathizers looking for Royalist fugitives. Any suspect who refused to accept Puritan ways, or Catholic who refused to accept their Protestant religion, was arrested and thrown into jail.

That Oliver Cromwell invented the term 'foolscap' paper? Before the demise of Charles I, paper-making in England was licensed by the king. Every sheet of paper produced carried the royal cypher (or monogram) as a watermark, visible when held up to the light. With his customary contempt for all things royal, Cromwell abolished the royal insignia and replaced it with the cap of a jester, i.e. a 'fools cap'. Before the advent of metric paper sizes, sheets of typing paper (regardless of the watermark) were known as foolscap.

How the Quakers got their name? The Quakers, originally known as the Children of Light (and now known as the Society of Friends) were founded around the mid-17th century by George Fox. They began as a sect of Protestant extremists, with views even more radical than the Puritans. On one occasion in 1650 Fox appeared in court accused of illegal preaching. He defended himself by saying that the judge, not he, would incur God's wrath. To which the judge replied that he was not afraid and that the only 'quaker' in court was Fox himself. The term stuck. There is an alternative version that says the name is derived from believers quaking with religious fervour during prayer readings.

That the fate of Charles I was predicted 100 years before? The 16th-century French prophet, Nostradamus, accurately predicted the outcome of the Civil War in several separate predictions, written in verse. They concern Charles I, Cromwell and Archbishop Laud. In one passage he wrote: *'The Parliament of London will put their king to death. He will die because of the shaven heads in council'*. He also foretold the Great Fire of London and gave the precise date of 1666. His predictions were all the more uncanny because they were made 100 years before the event.

ACKNOWLEDGEMENTS

We would like to thank: Graham Rich, Hazel Poole and Elizabeth Wiggans for their assistance.

Copyright © 1998 ticktock Publishing Ltd.

First published in Great Britain by ticktock Publishing Ltd., The Offices in the Square, Hadlow, Tonbridge, Kent, TN11 0DD. All rights reserved.

No part of this publication may be reproduced, stored in a retrieval system, or transmitted in any form or by any means electronic, mechanical, photocopying, recording or otherwise, without prior written permission of the copyright owner.

A CIP catalogue record for this book is available from the British Library. ISBN 1 86007 088 4

Picture research by Image Select.

Printed in Italy.

Picture Credits:

t=top, b=bottom, c=centre, l=left, r=right, OFC=outside front cover, IFC=inside front cover, OBC=outside back cover, IBC=inside back cover

AKG photo; 6bl, 23br. Ancient Art & Architecture Collection Ltd; 12bl, 13bl. Ann Ronan at Image Select; 10c, 14tl, 15br, 16/17c & OFC, 22/23ct, 26tl, 26b, 27tr, 27br & OFC. Ann Ronan Picture Library; 4/5b , 8tl & OBC, 11tr, 25b, 27bc, 27tc, 26/27c & OFC. The Bridgeman Art Library; OFC (main pic), 2/3t, 2bc, 4/5t, 4tl, 4bl, 6tl, 6/7c, 7br, 8/9 (main pic), 9tr, 10/11c, 10tl, 10tr, 10br, 11b, 12tl, 13br, 13tr, 14bl, 16tr, 19tr & OBC, 19br & OFC, 22bl, 25tr, 30/31t & IFC. CFCL/Image Select; 18bc, 24/25c. English Heritage; 7tc. e.t.archive; 17tr, 29c. Fotomas; 2tl, 3br, 5tr, 7c, 14/15cb, 15tr, 16c, 17br, 18tl, 20tc, 22tl, 21tr, 22bl, 22/23, 24cl, 28bl, 28/29c, 30c, 30/31c, 31bl. Geremy Butler Photography; 14/15c. Huntingdonshire District Council; 20bl. Image Select; 9cl, 16bl, 19tl & OBC, 24b, 30bc. J.Allan Cash Ltd; 5br, 32ct & OFC. Mary Evans Photo Library; 3tr, 12/13, 21b, 22/23c, 28br, 28tr, 28/29t, 31cr, OBC. National Maritime Museum; OBC (armillary sphere). Telegraph Colour Library; 16tl. Woodmansterne/Museum of London; 2/3b, 20/21.

Every effort has been made to trace the copyright holders and we apologize in advance for any unintentional omissions.
We would be pleased to insert the appropriate acknowledgement in any subsequent edition of this publication.

snapping-turtle
guide